CW01642268

A simple guide to Easy & Effective Enemas

Susie Tinson

A simple guide to Easy & Effective Enemas
© Susie Tinson

All rights reserved. No part of this publication may be reproduced, stored in any retrieval system or transmitted in any form or by any means, electronic, mechanical, photocopying, recording or otherwise, without the prior written permission of the copyright holder for which application should be addressed in the first instance to the publishers. No liability shall be attached to the author, the copyright holder or the publishers for loss or damage of any nature suffered as a result of the reliance on the reproduction of any of the contents of this publication or any errors or omissions in the contents.

The material in this book has been written and published solely for educational purposes. The intention of the author is to offer information of a general nature to help the reader in a quest for well-being. Statements made in this book and opinions expressed are those of the author and do not necessarily reflect the opinion or policy of publishers, Tricorn Books or the employing organisation, unless specifically stated.

The book and its contents are not intended to diagnose, treat or cure any infection, injury, illness or disease. Results can vary and each person's experience is unique. Please consult your health practitioner if you are in any doubt about any aspect of your health.

CONTRAINDICATIONS – Enemas should not be performed during pregnancy or while trying to get pregnant. Also please be careful if you have haemorrhoids.

ISBN 9781914615559

A CIP catalogue record for this book is available from the British Library

Published 2023 Tricorn Books
Aspex, Vulcan Building, Gunwharf Quays, Portsmouth PO1

Printed in UK

A simple guide to Easy & Effective Enemas

This book is dedicated to

My beautiful Mum who inspired me with her own health journey. Thank you Mum x

'Of all the polite topics of conversation, the state of one's intestines is probably at the bottom of most people's lists. Let's face it, irritable bowel syndrome, constipation, gas, diverticulitis and colon cancer are simply not things we like to discuss. And yet, as the old expression goes, death begins in the colon. Don't believe it? Ask any coroner. Autopsies often reveal colons that are plugged up to 80 percent with waste material.'

Vegetarian Times, March 1998

Many health imbalances such as constipation, chronic fatigue, depression and migraines can all benefit from cleansing the colon and the liver.

Leading such busy lives as most of us do these days, it is so easy to forget to look after ourselves in the way that we should. In the real world most of us do not have nutritionists, fitness coaches or health experts on hand to guide us in the right direction and therefore the only person managing us, is ourselves. So if you have been searching for answers to some of your health challenges then this book may be a very good starting point.

Easy Effective Enemas has been written in an easy-to-understand format by someone who has personally experienced and benefitted from the process, in the hope that it will inspire anyone who has a desire to improve their health and wellbeing.

CONTENTS –

Why would it be necessary to do an enema?	11
Diagram of a healthy colon	16
Diagram of an unhealthy colon	17
The Bristol Stool Chart	20
My Enema Story	21
Equipment required	23
The Enema procedure	28
Bowel Time	33
Other Enema Options/Additions	34
Juicing	41
Colonics	42
An important note on Hydration	44
EFA's (Essential Fatty Acids)	46
Suggested suppliers and References	48
Recommended further reading	49

WHY WOULD IT BE NECESSARY TO DO AN ENEMA?

Enemas are a wonderful and simple aid which can easily be used to gently assist our bodies to eliminate waste effectively and efficiently when needed. We regularly wash the outside, but seldom do we consider cleaning the inside of our bodies, but cleaning our internal pipes can actually help our health immensely. Some say that the body naturally cleanses itself so there should be no need for additional assistance and I agree, in an ideal world that should happen. But unfortunately, we don't live natural lives anymore and often our systems begin to break down from poor diet and poor elimination as well as from the continual daily onslaught of pollutants and toxins from our environment which then create a build-up. All of this makes it quite hard for the body to deal with, so we can begin to feel unwell.

This can put our body into a state of defence rather than into a state of growth and repair. Being in growth and repair is critical if we wish to remain healthy and strong because being in a state of defence or on high alert all the time is stressful for the body in the long term. It means that the body cannot give any energy to vital cleansing and healing which is very much needed to keep the body healthy and in balance.

In today's world we are constantly being bombarded from many different levels and so it has become practically unavoidable. Pollutants can come from many sources, but they are not always obvious, such as in the air that we breathe, which is not as clean as it used to be, especially in larger towns and cities. Chemicals and additives can also be found in our food either from being added during the manufacturing processes or from herbicides, fungicides and pesticides being sprayed onto crops when they are grown, especially if not organic. Even our tap water may contain many chemicals and drug residues which are not always filtered out at source and so we can unwittingly ingest them.

We also tend to lead much busier and more stressful lives than we did years ago and this can lead to a slow build-up of toxicity in our bodies, because continual stress creates acidity within our cells and stress is the most dehydrating thing of all for our health. One way to help heal the body is to remove, or at least try to minimise as much stress as possible and to also increase hydration.

We spend much more time indoors and in our homes than we used to, so can be surrounded by chemicals like flame retardants which are used during the manufacturing process on new items such as carpets, curtains and upholstery. These products continue to release residues and fumes for many months into the air that we breathe and are worsened if windows are not opened on a daily basis.

Most cleaning products contain harsh chemicals which are toxic if we breathe them in or get them onto our skin. Toiletries, many of which contain chemical additives like sulphates or artificial scents are easily absorbed through our skin, which in fact is our largest organ and can absorb up to 70% of what we put onto it. Deodorants often contain aluminium which is also harmful to health.

New clothes, unless they are organic, contain chemicals from the manufacturing processes, so I highly recommend washing brand new clothes before wearing them.

A new car has dozens of chemicals in its many components that can continually 'off gas' for many months and we breathe these in as we drive. These chemicals are intensified, even more so, by the heat of the sun on them. Driving can also mean inhaling fumes especially in traffic jams and while driving in towns. We all know how awful it feels to be stuck behind a vehicle that is chucking out poisonous fumes from its exhaust!

Perfumes, colognes, scented candles and plug in scents all give off chemical smells and residues which are toxic to the body, unless they are of a more natural origin such as containing essential oils or specifically stating they are natural or organically made. Some people can be very sensitive to these types of chemicals, often known as MCS (Multiple Chemical Sensitivity) which can create nausea, headaches, migraines, sweating and fatigue. For those with a high level of this kind of sensitivity, it can be very overwhelming going into shops, perfume departments, duty free areas etc., where there are thousands of new products all emitting strong chemical smells. Dry cleaning is another very toxic process and the scented sheets sometimes used in tumble driers are also unhealthy for the body.

It has been well documented that smoking is another pollutant, not only for the smoker but also for anyone inhaling that second hand smoke.

There are so many factors to consider when we look at improving our health which may include more exercise, better sleep patterns and good hydration along with positive changes of diet, or by reducing stress.

Our diet plays a huge part in our wellbeing. Eating habits have changed massively over the past 60 years or so. Our ancestors led a much simpler life with a plainer diet which was usually cooked from scratch. They would eat to live rather than live to eat! Today we enjoy such an abundance of choice and accessibility to different cultures and lifestyles, so our diets are much more diverse. We eat larger quantities so again our bodies have had to adapt and there are of course consequences to our digestions in consuming more complex foods.

Many people consume more alcohol and coffee which are actually very dehydrating to the body and in addition to this, much more sugar and carbohydrates, all of which are very acidifying. By then eating far too little fruit and vegetables than is really healthy, the body is not helped to balance these things out. In the UK it is well accepted that five portions a day is the number to aim for but few even achieve that. Surprisingly, many other countries have much higher targets. For example in Japan the recommended total is 17 portions of fruit and vegetables per day!

So we can begin to see how easily our bodies are being hugely challenged on a daily basis to try to keep us in a balanced state so that we can function normally. It is imperative that our body finds ways to store these toxins somewhere safely in order to literally keep us safe and alive! It's a bit like continually filling the rubbish bin in your kitchen. If you don't take the rubbish out regularly then it will overflow, the kitchen will eventually become so full of rubbish that there is no room left to manoeuvre. It is exactly the same with our bodies, the toxicity builds slowly over time so that we don't notice it at first, but eventually it will begin to give out some signals that all is not happy within. These signals and symptoms are an early warning sign that our body is having a problem and needs some attention! Ignoring these early signs will lead to bigger alerts until eventually something breaks down.

However, with all of that said, the human body is supremely intelligent and contrary to popular belief, will never actually work against us. Instead it will constantly try to find ways to eliminate through all of the usual routes such as the bowel, the urine, through expiration of our lungs or via the skin (sweating). If these routes are not possible, then our bodies will begin to store the toxicity away from our vital organs in order to protect us. One of the easiest ways it can do this is to pack the toxins into our fat cells in various areas to keep us safer in the short term which seems a good idea. However, this is a bit of a trade-off because over time, as the body begins to struggle to keep up with the overspill, little niggles start to appear, such as headaches, bloating, aches and pains, tiredness, joint pain or skin problems which indicate that all is not well deep inside. These are some of the initial warning signs that tell us our bodies need help to relieve the pressure that is slowly building up.

In an ideal world our body should naturally be eliminating at least 70% of its waste via the colon, but if it cannot do that efficiently, then over time it is likely that not only will we begin to feel much more sluggish, tired or irritable and maybe even lack motivation, but potentially could even begin to develop other more serious symptoms of disease in the future.

So how do we begin to alleviate much of the above and more?

It makes really good sense to give our bodies a helping hand sometimes. Enemas can help us to do this because they offer an opportunity for our body to release waste which relieves the pressure, thereby creating some much needed space again. Once we begin to feel better we can think more clearly, which enables us to make better health choices.

To give you an idea of what I am talking about, here are two examples of both a healthy and an unhealthy colon –

THIS IS WHAT A HEALTHY COLON SHOULD LOOK LIKE: –

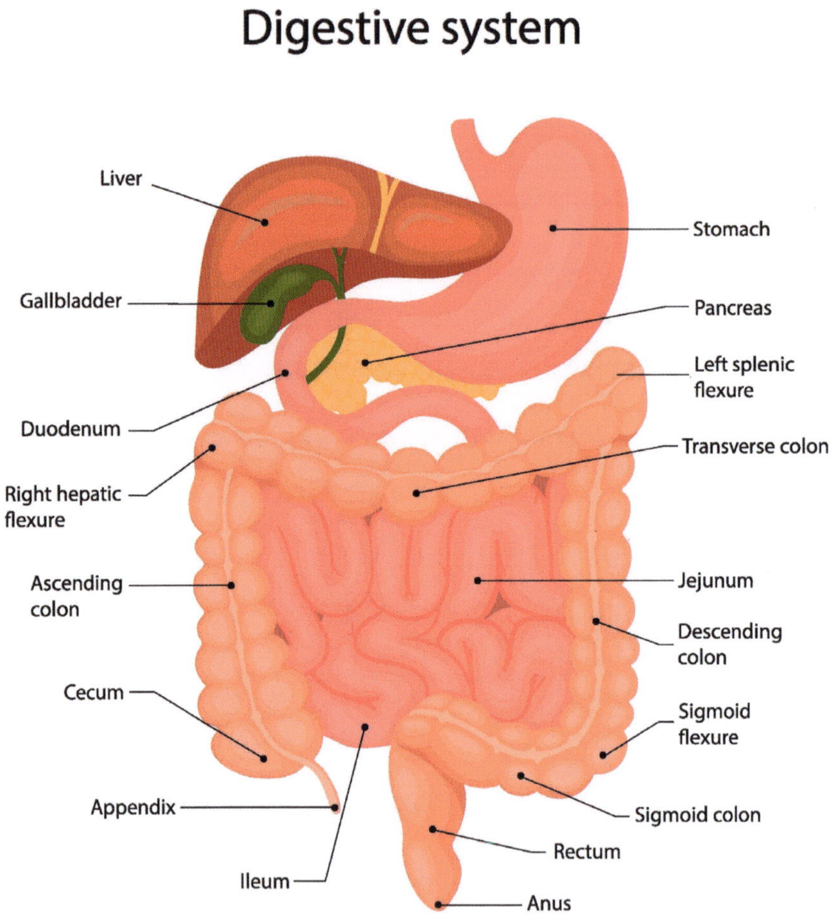

THIS IS AN UNHEALTHY COLON –

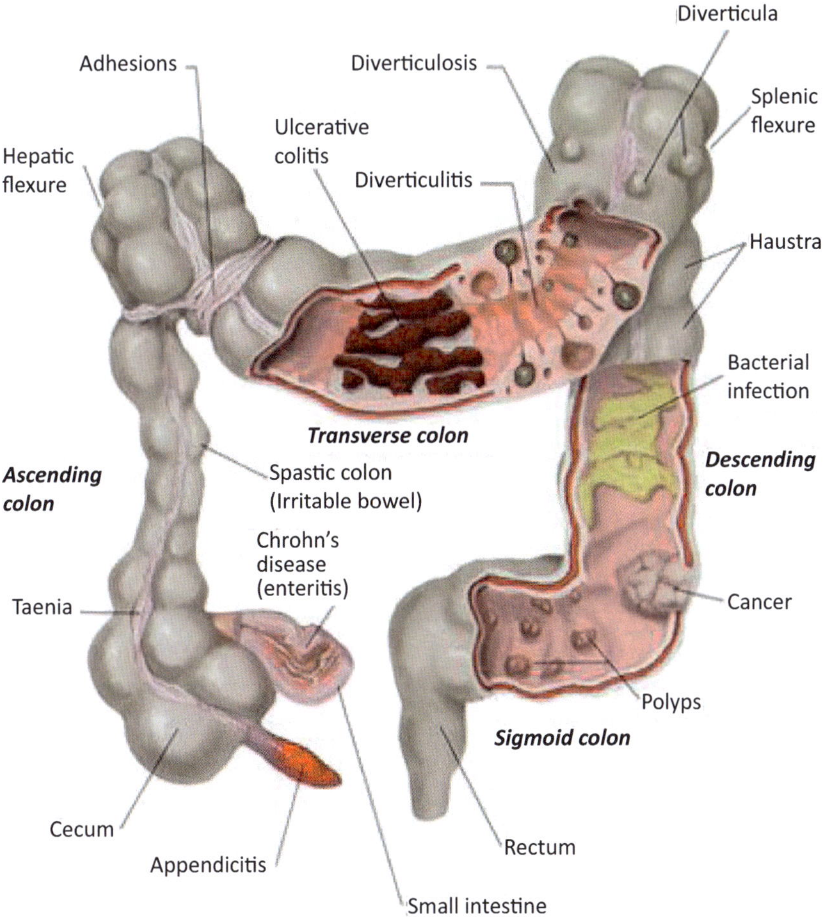

You can see that the unhealthy colon is very misshapen and looks sickly. Some signs of an unhealthy colon include poor complexion, blemishes, acne, bloating, gas, fatigue, constipation and haemorrhoids. But over time these can easily be corrected.

Enemas help to improve and regain the muscle tone in the colon and to stimulate all of the reflexes in the intestines. They also help to support and treat the liver which is really important as the liver does much of the hard work in our bodies.

Although some may find it quite a strange idea to use a tube to introduce water internally to cleanse, there is actually nothing abnormal or unusual about doing enemas and they are not a new phenomenon. In fact, enemas have been around for hundreds of years and there are even references to them being used as far back as biblical times, albeit in a very basic way. In more recent years, enemas were quite common practice in hospitals and one of the first things a doctor might have prescribed or a nurse might administer, was an enema to clean out some of the backlog in the colon to prepare for things such as surgery or child birth. During these times, enemas were considered quite routine and were used alongside other simple natural strategies such as putting patients outside into the sunshine to obtain natural vitamin D and to get some fresh air and oxygen to help the healing process along. Many of these basic principles were used as an important aid to boost the immune system so that the patient would heal more quickly. Such options, combined with a good diet and good general care were actually very successful in helping patients to regain their health and were not only cheap but extremely effective.

Unfortunately, many of these simple strategies have either been lost or forgotten by the masses and treatments such as enemas are now frowned upon, feared or often rejected as abnormal or strange because most of us have never been introduced to them. However, they can be very useful in helping to relieve many conditions such as constipation, headaches/migraines, irritable bowel syndrome, painful periods, bloating, gas and so many more. In addition to relieving some of these uncomfortable issues, performing enemas on a regular basis, as mentioned above, could even potentially be helpful in preventing a much more serious disease in the future.

So let's take a brief look at what constitutes a healthy poo? A healthy poo is one that passes without straining and one where you don't feel the need to use lots of toilet paper, as it should come out fairly cleanly and easily and not be sticky. As a guide we should be eliminating on average 1-3 times every day and ideally after meals.

Here is a simple chart as a rough guide, known as The Bristol Stool Chart –

My Enema Story

Personally, I first came across enemas while staying at a health retreat and initially was one of those people who feared doing them. It was suggested that all participants try them as part of the detox programme we were on, but I was not at all excited by the idea! In fact, I felt very nervous and having listened to the talk and watched intently while the equipment was being demonstrated, I decided that I would leave it until I was back in the comfort of my own home. However, if I had made the effort to try one whilst at the retreat, I think I could have probably saved myself from experiencing some of the uncomfortable and unpleasant side effects that I experienced as part of my detox, especially the headaches. Plus I would have been able to share my experience with others going through a similar situation and ask questions, which are not always possible outside of these environments as it can be seen as a bit of a taboo subject!

Once back at home, I did eventually summon up the courage to try an enema, but without a book of instructions, I really didn't have a clue if I was doing it properly! There was no internet for information and not knowing anyone who had done an enema before, it certainly wasn't something that I felt comfortable to openly discuss with most people. So on my first attempt I wasn't even sure if the enema had been successful or not! In fact, any information I had received from the retreat seemed vague and confusing and the use of coffee had been encouraged without first doing a water flush which made it quite interesting, as it was far too powerful for a first experience! Although coffee enemas are fantastic, I would not suggest that anyone begin with a coffee enema. It's always best to start with a plain water flush first to see how the body responds and then to progress to coffee and perhaps also other additions later.

Since that initial experience, I've done many enemas either at home or at retreats and also when travelling and actually quite enjoy the experience now, finding them very effective as well as easy to perform. The benefits are well worth the small effort required. They can often bring such huge relief, literally instantly and can help you to feel much better just by energising and uplifting you or by clearing brain fog or relieving a headache.

One of the main reasons for writing this easy guide is because I've heard so many people on retreats say exactly the same things that I did when initially confronted with what seemed like a strange and unfamiliar procedure. Some of those reasons being, that they don t want to try them for fear of what might happen, that they don't have a clue what to do or that they just prefer to do it in the comfort of their own homes. However, I've discovered that once back at home, most people never seem to get around to it and the enema kit inevitably sits in the bottom of a drawer unused, which is such a shame. Some are also too afraid to ask what they see as silly questions and therefore miss out on such a beneficial tool which could help them to feel so much better and in the case of a detox, give massive relief from possible uncomfortable symptoms.

Although fantastic and hugely beneficial, enemas are not just for aiding and assisting comfort levels of a detox though. There are so many more reasons why you can benefit from them. For example, from the uncomfortable symptoms of jet lag, or during an illness like a cold, where an enema can often help to speed up the recovery time.

Doing an enema for yourself gives you such a beneficial aid that is so easy to do in the comfort of your own home, thereby putting you in control of your own health which is a powerful thing! Enema kits are cheap to buy and also easily available, so there's no expensive equipment to purchase. They are portable, and once you are used to doing them, you can easily have a mini enema travel kit already made up to take away with you. All you need once you get to your destination is some clean water such as filtered or bottled and you're away!

Once proficient with the process, you can then add different things to the water to give specific benefits for example, using coffee for detoxification or camomile, which is very soothing and calming, but more about these later on.

So, let's get to the important equipment and the 'How to do it' section –

EQUIPMENT REQUIRED

The equipment as already mentioned before, is very straightforward. It usually consists of either a bag or small bucket with a narrow tube attached to it and on this is a pinching clip that turns easily for controlling the rate of water flow into the body. Some kits come with an additional long douche attachment but these are not necessary for enemas.

Most kits look like this –

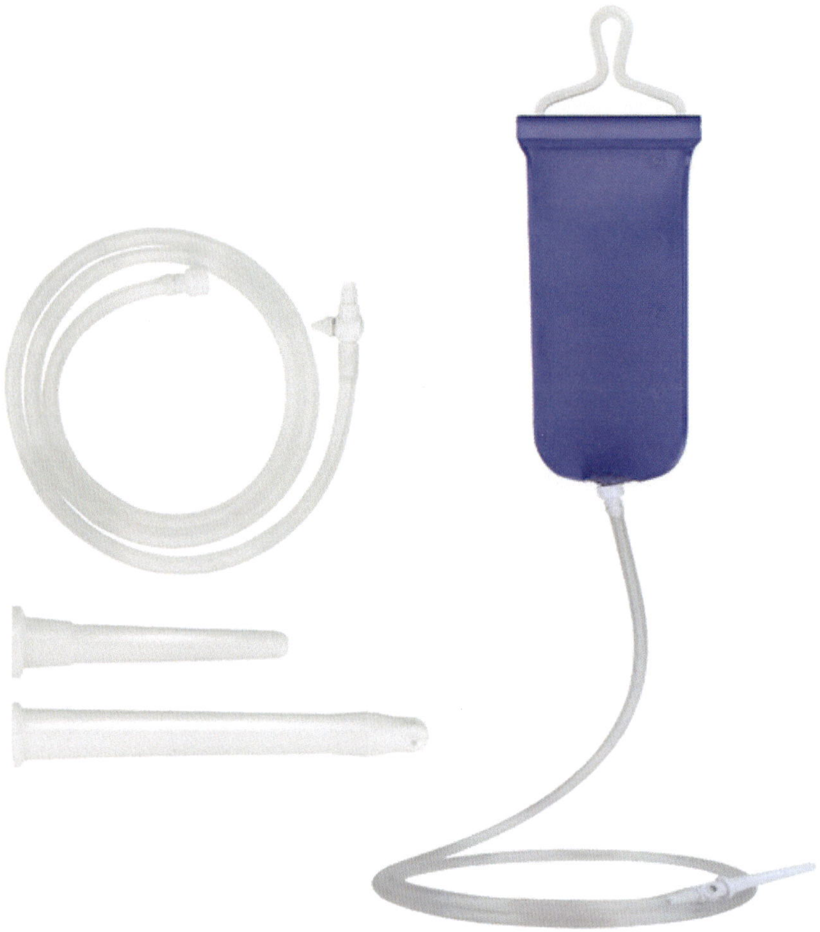

The bag systems are one of the easiest and cheapest forms of enema kits as they fold flat, making them simple to store away or to travel with. They are usually available from chemists or health shops and also can be found online.

You will need some sort of lubrication. One favoured option is almond oil, again available from chemists or health stores. In fact most chemists and health shops sell small sized bottles which are very easy for packing into your travel kit. Chickweed cream is another option and is both soothing and healing, particularly if you suffer from haemorrhoids. You could also use any simple vegetable oil/olive oil or coconut oil and make up your own little bottle. I tend to use coconut oil myself as it sets when cool so is easier for travelling, plus it is antimicrobial and antibacterial as well as soothing and moisturising on the skin.

Comfort levels are very important but this comes down to personal choice. I use an old towel which I keep specifically for the purpose of doing enemas. A blanket underneath will give some cushioning and warmth if on a hard floor. If you prefer something more waterproof on top or underneath the towel, you could use bed training pads from chemists or disabled shops. A colourful plastic square mat from baby shops, the type used under high chairs could also be used and certainly works well. A cushion for your head is a useful addition. But all of this said, it is possible to manage with just 1 small towel when travelling or when needing a quick treatment and if nothing else is available!

I usually have a kettle of hot water already boiled so that I can top up the enema bag with water again should it get too cold or if I want more for an additional fill, plus a jug of cold filtered water to get the temperature just right. These things don't matter too much but just saves having to go back to the kitchen!

Another very good but optional piece of equipment is a small stool. You can usually find these in online shops in various colours. Stools, designed for helping toddlers to reach the sink are a great choice but just make sure they are sturdy enough, although you won't actually put your full weight on it. They don't have to be very high. The reason for using a stool is to elevate your feet thereby creating more of a squat, which is actually the natural position for us to eliminate. Since the invention of the toilet, squatting is something few of us do these days, unless you have been abroad and had the wonderful experience of squatting over a large hole in the ground! In a squat position your legs are brought up to naturally squeeze the abdomen which gives a gentle massage and helps to encourage elimination. It also allows the bowels to relax more easily too, giving your body the signal that it is time to let go. But if no stool is available still do the enema!

The only other thing needed is a spare toilet roll or tissues to have next to you on the floor.

You can really go to town and create a nice calming space for yourself, making the process even more relaxing and enjoyable. For example a few nice natural candles rather than a harsh overhead light creates a lovely atmosphere. Having soft music playing in the background can be soothing too. A book or a magazine to distract and while away the time, but I usually quite enjoy the peace and actually just doing nothing during the process!

Performing an enema is really a very simple process. It can take as little as 15-30 minutes once you are familiar with the routine, but sometimes up to an hour depending on the time it takes you to set up and how many fills of water you personally need to do and whether you want to have additional enemas afterwards like coffee etc. But it's just a matter of listening to your body and if things don't go to plan the first time, you can stop and try again another day. There are no rules here just guidelines. I really want you to enjoy your experience and to feel the benefits. It is such a powerful, yet simple tool to master and well worth the effort to experience the great feeling of a successful treatment. Once the process is established, you will find it really easy to fit them into your routine.

So if this is your first time, get your enema bag out of its box and push the tubing onto the enema bag or bucket so it is secure, sometimes this is a screw fixing. Then add the smaller nozzle onto the other end, making sure it is firmly in place. Next check the height you are going to hang it. I usually hang mine from a door handle if it's not too high – around waist height is good to enable enough gravity. Some people have a hook on the wall especially for the purpose. You need to check the positioning of this in terms of where you will be lying. Good proximity to the toilet and ideally not with your head at the toilet end as it is all about practicalities here!

If you find it difficult getting up and down from the floor, it is possible to lie on a bench or even a bed – an inexpensive folding camp bed could work. You can buy press up benches like the type used in gyms or use a Colema board (which is another type of enema). These should all be available online. If you use one of these alternatives, remember to adjust the height of the enema bag accordingly.

THE ENEMA PROCEDURE –

First boil the kettle ready for filling the enema bag. The water you use is very important.

The idea behind doing enemas is to eliminate some of the toxicity in your body which may be giving you discomfort in the first place. So the last thing you want to do is to use ordinary tap water, which contains many chemical residues and will therefore introduce more unnecessary toxicity back into your body. So the best options are good quality filtered water such as reverse osmosis or a good bottled water. There are many good filters on the market but even a basic Brita filter is better than tap water! Bottled water is the obvious choice when travelling.

Next set up the space in your bathroom, make sure it's warm and comfortable and maybe have a spare blanket or extra towel to cover you just in case, it's all in the planning!

Check that the clamp on the enema tube is in the closed position then fill the enema bag to about a quarter with cold filtered water. Next add a little of the boiled water, maybe up to another quarter. Then keep adding more cold or hot water bit by bit checking the temperature until it has filled to about ¾ full. Test with your little finger, wrist or elbow to find the comfortable temperature – body temperature is best. It is better for the water to be slightly too cool than too hot, otherwise it can be very uncomfortable for your insides and you certainly don't want a burnt bottom! Blood temperature is about right. There is no need to fill the enema bag right to the top as it's easy to spill if you accidentally squeeze it too hard while hooking it up!

Hook the enema bag into position, making sure it is very secure. With the nozzle held over the loo, bath or sink, open the valve and let a little of the water out. This is to eliminate any air bubbles as you don't want to introduce air into your body especially if you are already a little gassy! You should be able to see any air pockets in the tube as they move out. Tapping the tube can release any that remain. Then turn the nozzle back to the off position, which is normally horizontal.

Remove your lower clothes and lie on the floor. (I apologise for stating what seem like obvious and basic instructions, especially for those who may already be familiar, but incredibly I've heard amusing stories from people who did not remove their lower half of clothing with very interesting results!! So I wanted to be super clear on every instruction to avoid any possible confusion or omission. Once you are familiar with the process you probably won't need these instructions anyway!

With the lubricant, take a small fingertip amount and lubricate the tip of the enema tube. (If you feel you need additional help, you can also lubricate your anus but it's not usually necessary.) Lying on your side, left is sometimes preferable, with your knees up. Begin to slowly insert the tip of the tube into your bottom. Feed the tube further in bit by bit until it is approximately a couple of inches inside you – no more. There should never be any pain. If there is any resistance that is fine, you can leave the tube where it stops. It may be that you have hit an air bubble or some solid matter. In this instance you may find that only a small amount of water will go in which is fine. Next time it will go further. If you find inserting while lying on your left side awkward then this may not be the best position for you. There is no wrong or right way to do this it's about whatever is the most comfortable and practical for you. We are all different shapes and sizes so you can either try the right side or you can lie on your back and insert the tube with your hand between your legs. Alternatively you can go onto all fours and then by leaning on one elbow insert with the other hand behind you.

Whichever way you choose (and you may find a position that suits you better than these), please take your time and insert slowly without any jarring movements as the tissues inside of the anus are delicate. Also be mindful of any haemorrhoids. Once you feel the tube is comfortably in place, regardless of position, I suggest you come onto your left side for the first fill, which is comfortable for most people, if not, move onto your back. After the first fill and once you are proficient you can adjust the insert position and also manoeuvre your position on the floor once the tube is out, so that you feel comfortable. For the first fill though, I suggest you remain on your left side as you will probably find this easier to get up for the first time to the loo.

Slowly turn the valve to open and let in some of the water gently. If at any time you feel the flow is going in too fast or you just want to rest, you can turn the valve off or pinch the tube between finger and thumb to slow it down. My suggestion is to take it slowly and for your first time maybe only put a small amount of water inside – perhaps as much as ¼ of the bag to see how your body feels and to gauge the reaction. Once you are feeling more confident you can always let more in. It's also perfectly ok to let all of the bag in at once if you choose to, but again only if you feel comfortable to do this. Let the water sit for a minute or so inside you and again see how that feels. You can then let a little more water in if it feels right. Once you are OK with the amount you want to retain, pull the tube slowly out of your bottom and lay it on a tissue or the side of the towel/ mat you are lying on.

You may feel an immediate urge to let go, if so don't worry about holding onto it, just begin clenching your buttocks and get up and shuffle to the loo as the urge may be strong. Sit on the toilet, ideally with your feet on the stool. Once you feel you have released completely, you can begin the process again.

For subsequent fills, (after initially beginning on your left side), and once the tube has been removed, manoeuvre onto your back if you are not already in that position.

You can then gently begin to massage your tummy. You don't have to do this every time but when you do, it's best to start from the lower right hand side of the abdomen and slowly work your way up the right side of your tummy, across the top (a couple of inches below the ribcage) and then down the left hand side, this follows the contour of the colon and will encourage a release. You can also massage your tummy while sitting on the toilet. Massaging in small circular motions, pressing with your fingers or very gently with your fist. This again may encourage a further elimination. In your mind say the words "release, release" or "let go, let go" It may surprise you how the body responds when you do this!

Regular massage of the tummy area is a good thing to do generally at any time and particularly in the morning before getting up. Also getting into the habit of giving your tummy a gentle massage while sitting on the toilet will help to encourage your body into a good routine of eliminating. The only exception would be just after a meal when the body is digesting and then it's best to leave a good two hours after eating to allow that process to complete.

After you have done several fills and several empties you should begin to see the water running clear from you. Once this happens, you will know that it's time to cease the treatment. But of course you can finish the treatment at any point before this if it feels more comfortable to do so.

Once you have completed the enema process, there will still be a little water in the tube. Hold the enema kit high to give some gravity and let the remaining water out into the toilet or bath then secure the nozzle back into the off position ready for next time. Clean the nozzle with hot soapy water and then hang the kit up to dry. If you feel you would like to use something stronger, then I suggest going the natural route. Periodically I use a product called Germ-a-clenz to spray around the end of the nozzle. It's made by The American herb and Spice Company and is an amazing natural product made of pure oregano oil. I've used it for many years for this purpose and I also use it in other areas of my home for sterilizing and cleaning generally. It is safe and non-toxic, but is also anti-bacterial, anti-microbial, and anti-fungal so it can be used to wipe around the bathroom. Occasionally I put a couple of sprays into the enema bag before flushing out thoroughly with plenty of water especially if I haven't used the bag for a while as this will help to reduce any issues like mould, bacteria etc. Just be sure to rinse the bag thoroughly after spraying as although it's perfectly safe, it is quite a strong herb. It has so many uses and is one product I was so glad to discover, especially when I threw out all my nasty chemical cleaning products and wondered what on earth I would use in their place! There are of course many other natural cleaning products on the market to try. Products containing tea tree oil are another good natural option. I love tea tree hand soaps. Or you can easily add a drop or two of essential oils like oregano/tea tree to some hand soap to add that additional freshness or sterilizing effect. Products used to sterilise baby bottles would be another option if you prefer to use a much stronger less natural product.

Bowel time –

In Chinese medicine they see different parts of the body as corresponding to a 2 hour time slot on the 24 hour clock. For example, between the hours of 5am - 7am is known as bowel time and is the perfect elimination time. So if you are an early riser, it is really good to encourage your body to maximise this opportunity at a time when it would naturally want to co-operate more easily and is therefore also a great time for doing an enema. It is perfectly safe and again beneficial to do an enema straight after your first morning bowel movement to encourage a further elimination. You will know if your body is happy to co-operate and it can really set you up for the day by giving a little energy boost.

OTHER ENEMA OPTIONS/ADDITIONS –

Camomile –

Once you feel confident with water enemas, there are some other options which can be added to the treatment to benefit your body. For example once you have done an initial water flush, you can do another fill of camomile tea if you would like to relax further. Camomile is very useful for soothing the bowel. If you have trouble drifting off to sleep easily, a camomile enema can be useful to encourage deep relaxation before bedtime. Enemas are generally best done in the morning but a camomile enema is a great option for evening. Camomile is also good for the liver and is a more gentle option than using a coffee enema to cleanse. Using 2 camomile tea bags make up half a pint with boiling water and let it steep for 10 minutes. Then add cold water to the required temperature. You can also use dried organic camomile flowers – 2 tablespoons infused in 16oz of boiling water for 10-15 minutes, strained and cooled to body temperature.

Linseed water and Linseed Tea –

Many people are dehydrated so for additional hydration, linseed water is a great option. Add a couple of tablespoons of linseeds to a mug and fill with boiling water, leave overnight and then use the liquid only in an enema bag with additional warm water (not the seeds – these can be added to muesli or smoothies for even greater benefit from hydration and fibre).

Linseed tea is similar to linseed water but even more hydrating. Soak 2 tablespoons of linseed overnight, then pour the seeds and the water into a saucepan in the morning and add an additional litre of water, bring to the boil (make sure it doesn't boil over) and then simmer for one hour, turn off and leave to cool. Strain, then add a cupful of the liquid to an enema bag and top up with warm water. This is an incredibly soothing and hydrating enema to do and is great for anyone that is severely dehydrated or constipated or had an episode of diarrhoea, or been poorly and is in much need of hydration.

Homeopathic Remedies –

Homeopathic remedies can also be added to enema bags if required and are absorbed easily. Just dissolve them into the warm (not hot) water.

Aloe Vera –

Aloe Vera is wonderfully soothing and healing and can be added along with the water. It's great for inflammation and pain, also soothing for haemorrhoids and is a wonderful addition for hydration. Try to find a pure Aloe Vera liquid that has none or very few additives. It can be used neat as well as diluted – a couple of tablespoons added to an enema bag with some warm water should be sufficient.

Chlorophyll implant –

Using freshly squeezed green juice either straight or mixed with water is both nourishing and calming.

Probiotics –

To help replenish or to encourage healthy gut bacteria probiotics are a very useful addition especially if suffering from wind. If you have had a tummy upset or recently taken a course of antibiotics, then taking some probiotics orally or rectally is very helpful.

1-2 teaspoons of powder in lukewarm water should be sufficient in an enema.

Flax oil –

Joanna Budwig was a scientist who discovered that Flax oil enemas can help to alleviate toxins from the body and often treated her patients with flax oil enemas to help in more serious situations like cancer. She discovered that Flax oil remarkably brings light, energy and healing into the body. Some of the high metals that we may have absorbed such as mercury from fillings, lead and aluminium from our environment and even toxins from pharmaceutical drugs are usually stored away in our fat cells. So how do we access those? The use of flax oil by enema introduces light and 'jump starts' all of the cells in the body, awakening them and amazingly floods them with vitality, literally bringing them to life! Udo Erasmus author of "Fats that heal, fats that kill" discovered that once the oil is in the colon, it is able to absorb fat soluble toxins via the lymphatic system and then the oil carries them out of the body once it's eliminated. So flax oil enemas flood the body with light and also help to remove toxicity out at the same time, so that our cells get a little boost in energy and can operate more healthily and freely again. Now how amazing is that?!

How to do a Flax oil enema –

You will need 250ml of organic flax oil and a folded towel for protecting your bed.

It is best to do a water flush first to make sure the bowel is clear and also helps the retention of the oil. You can release this water straight away.

Next mix 250ml of organic flax/linseed oil with 100ml of warm water in a small saucepan and bring this mixture to body temperature (test with your little finger). Pour the oil and water into the enema bag. The oil and water will separate. Open the clip and let the water run down and out of the tube into the toilet. Turn if off when the oil appears in the tube so that only the water is lost. Insert the oil rectally, just the same as if doing a basic enema, lying on your back or on your side on an old towel. The difference in doing an oil enema is that you may be surprised at how your body will readily take the oil in without the need to stop halfway as it recognises the potential of this beautiful oil. It should feel very soothing.

You can now go and lay on your bed for up to an hour. The oil should be easy to hold as the body will enjoy the photon exchange of light and colour. This is a great time to do a guided meditation, many of which can easily be found online or just rest and enjoy the peace, visualizing the light coming into your body.

After 1 hour go and release the oil, although you may find that your body is happy to hold onto it for longer! So it's a good idea to stay indoors close to a bathroom until you feel confident that it's all been released. However, if you do need to go out then do a warm water flush to eliminate any remaining oil. You may want to line your pants if you are going out and also that night if you have done the Flax enema close to bedtime as sometimes a little oil may seep out especially if you accidentally pass wind! If there's been no movement of oil after 1-2 hours it is a good idea to do a simple water flush enema. In addition, the next day is an excellent time to do a coffee enema to encourage a further release and to make sure that all the metals have exited the body.

Coffee –

The benefits of coffee enemas were discovered during World War 1 by overworked, over tired nurses who poured coffee into an enema bag in a desperate attempt to help relieve the pain of soldiers after surgery. There were shortages of painkillers such as morphine and surgeons only had enough available to help patients through surgery but not for post-operative pain. Many of the soldiers were prescribed enemas for constipation but they reported that having the extra coffee enemas gave them pain relief.

Coffee enemas help to open and clear the liver and are very popular particularly with people who follow the Gerson therapy, where they are performed on a daily basis for a period of time to stimulate the liver to dump more toxins for healing purposes. This happens because the coffee utilizes the pathway via the portal vein system in the rectal area. The body then drives it directly to the liver where the bile ducts are triggered by the caffeine to release bile enabling the liver to dump toxins, which ultimately helps to take the pressure off the liver. By doing this process, uncomfortable problems like headaches, nausea and pain can be alleviated. Even if you don't drink coffee, taking it rectally will not have the same effect on your body as drinking it and is therefore not a problem for most people who wish to avoid caffeine for health reasons.

It is essential to use a good quality organic coffee for the enema. Unroasted is milder and it must be organic as coffee is a heavily sprayed crop. Specific enema coffees are available online, the Gerson being one of them. 1 tablespoon in 1 litre of water is usually sufficient. Bring it to a boil on the stove (in a non-aluminium pan) then let it simmer for 20 minutes and turn it off, let it cool and strain before use in case of any stray grains. It is therefore best prepared a few hours ahead as it can then be warmed back up by having boiling water added to reach the desired temperature and make up to approximately 2 litres of coffee solution. Use less coffee or dilute more if you think you may be sensitive, so you can see how your body reacts to the first experience. Any sign of sensitivity like palpitations when taking coffee enemas for the first time are usually a sign of toxicity and this should settle down after a few treatments as the liver begins to clear.

For the purpose of coffee enemas, these are best taken when lying on your right side rather than the left as there is better absorption into the mesenteric veins on this side. From these veins the caffeine is then absorbed into the portal system more easily.

It may not be possible to do this, but if you can, try to hold the coffee for up to 15 minutes as the blood goes through the liver every 3 minutes and the coffee helps the blood flow to increase, which helps to remove the toxins and eliminate them through the bowel. So coffee enemas are a blood cleanser.

Coffee enemas are powerful, so are very good in helping to assist the detoxification and healing process. An excellent time to do a coffee enema is on a full moon as the blood tends to be thicker and stickier around this time which can make us feel pain, have skin flare ups or be more tired and irritable. So a coffee enema helps to relieve the toxicity that is causing the discomfort.

If you are thirsty after a coffee enema, which does sometimes happen as they can be a little drying, then do make sure you rehydrate well and drink plenty of water. Having a green juice after an enema is excellent to rebalance the electrolytes.

Both the Gerson Institute and The Hippocrates Health Institute in Florida highly recommend water as well as coffee or wheatgrass enemas as a daily habit on their programmes and particularly in the initial stages of cleansing and healing our bodies. Daily water enemas and weekly coffee enemas are a good idea for most people, particularly if you have never done them before, or never had a colonic and you think you may have years of accumulated matter sitting inside you. Some people have the equivalent of up to 8 meals sitting inside their colons!! So if your diet has been very poor, or you have had long periods of constipation, for which you have had to take suppositories or laxatives to help you eliminate, then you may well find that doing frequent enemas initially can bring about positive changes in your bowel regularity. Also if you are doing a detox or are on any cleansing diet, it's a great idea to add the enemas in for extra assistance. You will definitely notice the difference!

After a few weeks you can ease off to possibly once a week or whenever you feel there will be some positive benefit to doing an enema.

JUICING –

I have often done enemas or had colonics as part of a juicing plan or similar protocol either at home or in retreats. Enemas and particularly coffee enemas sit very well alongside juicing. This is because juicing gives the body a chance to rest from digestion while enemas/coffee enemas and colonics clear space. Juicing floods the body with electrolytes which help to keep things like our PH levels in balance. Juicing with organic fruits and vegetables is very cleansing and will flood the cells with an abundance of nutrition, vitamins and minerals which encourages the cells to release toxins. The enemas and coffee enemas are then very useful for taking that toxicity safely out of the body quickly and efficiently and therefore helping to minimise any side effects such as headaches. It's a great re-set for the body and can leave you feeling re-energised and full of vitality. I usually aim for 4-5 juices a day (or 2-3 litres) and ideally with a good amount of green produce which is very alkalising. Green juices are great to have straight after a coffee enema for rebalancing the electrolytes. Spring is one of the best times for juicing and in fact any time from the spring equinox onwards is perfect as the rising spring energy supports this process more easily, rather than during the colder winter months when we are still hibernating and favouring more warm and grounding foods such as soups and stews etc.

Basic green juice recipe – using organic produce.

Juice 1 green apple (or apple of choice), 2 sticks of celery, half a lemon or lime including the rind, half a cucumber, some lettuce leaves, chunk of ginger, some herbs like parsley or mint. Then strain and drink within 20 minutes of juicing to receive all of the lovely goodness.

COLONICS –

May I also suggest that in addition to fairly regular enemas, you also consider having some Colonic Hydro-Therapy. Colonics really are fantastic at clearing debris much deeper into the colon. As a bare minimum, I'd suggest a colonic in the springtime to cleanse after the long winter months. Around the spring equinox in March is a brilliant time, especially as the body naturally wants to shed layers at this time of the year. So whether that means shedding layers of clothes or layers of fat, or dust and clutter when we like to spring clean our homes, it also makes good sense to clear some of the internal layers that we may have accumulated over the winter months owing to heavier and denser diets and less activity. Another very good time for a colonic is at the end of the summer, to prepare for the winter, around September/October. The autumn equinox is therefore an ideal time for cleansing and colonics too. There can be so many benefits if you get into this practice regularly. It gives the body a lovely boost in the spring time when the energy is rising, but also can give a head start for the autumn/winter, before all the heavier foods come back into your diet. Colonics provide another very valuable tool to help you stay on top of your health.

I have phases when I have colonics every couple of months, especially if doing some cleansing or changing my diet. They are a great kick start to any new routine. In fact if you are inclined to, having one would give you a great head start to deep clean the body and release some of the layers before you embark on doing enemas regularly at home. Some therapists will recommend a course of several colonics if there have been years of accumulation in the bowel or if there is a niggling health issue such as hay fever. It really is quite incredible to observe the results and to experience the improvement of health that can be achieved by following this practice on a regular basis. Once you have had some colonics, enemas can then be used to periodically maintain the system.

An important note on HYDRATION –

Your body is made up of 70% water so drinking plenty of good quality water is vital to your health and whilst enemas and colonics will help to introduce some water to a dehydrated body, there really is no better cure than drinking plenty of good quality water on a regular basis. If you don't have flow you will stagnate. You have trillions of cells in your body that need to be able to move freely to function effectively. Many people are severely dehydrated but don't realise it. This creates issues in the body including constipation and constipation type headaches, tiredness and lethargy as well as pain. Dehydration is the beginning of so many health issues and long term dehydration can eventually lead to a much more serious disease. So hydration really is the beginning of the solution.

As the saying goes – "Dilution is the solution to pollution".

Drinking water, ideally in-between meals helps to flush out many of the toxins on a daily basis. Drinking tea, coffee or soft drinks is not completely hydrating. If you have not drunk much plain water for a long time, then begin very slowly. Your body will need to be retrained to enjoy water again. Monitor your intake and increase day by day. 1-2 litres is usually a good amount for most people in addition to teas and coffees etc. However we are all individual with different lifestyles so I suggest you initially aim for 1 litre increasing to 1.5 litres and eventually 2 litres and see how you feel. Keep a chart as you go along to monitor changes.... are you less tired, having less headaches, feeling more energised, have less aches and pain? It is a really interesting exercise to do and can bring many surprising changes. Eating more water rich foods like fruits, salads and vegetables and soups will also help to hydrate your body.

Drinking too much coffee and tea as well as alcohol can have dehydrating effects on the body, so by reducing these and adding in more herbal teas instead, along with drinking lots more pure water will help to redress the balance. You can always add some lemon or cucumber slices to the water if you don't like it plain. Coconut water with half a squeezed lime is very refreshing in hot weather.

Getting into the habit of drinking a glass of warm water first thing on waking with a slice/squeeze of lemon added, is a great kick start to the day for your liver and is also good for hydration.

Often our bodies confuse the signal for thirst with hunger so drinking a glass of water in between meals can massively help over time to give your body the message of hydration. A glass of water 20-30 minutes before a meal is a good idea rather than drinking water during a meal which can affect digestion and dilute important vitamins and minerals. However, drinking other beverages with a meal is fine.

Linseed water or Linseed teas as mentioned earlier are another great way to increase your hydration. Simply drinking the water from the soaked linseeds or adding some boiling water to half a mug of linseed tea is very soothing on a daily basis. I like to add the soaked linseeds (along with the water) to a smoothie each day or just the seeds on their own can be added to some muesli. Soaked linseeds help to get the bowels moving. They are also very soothing to the intestinal tract. So anyone who feels that their digestive tract is inflamed or sensitive or upset will find that the seeds and teas will help to calm things down.

Essential Fatty Acids –

Another important point to note is that the body also requires Essential Fatty Acids (EFA's) for so many of its processes. EFA's are the lubricant in the body and they really help to keep the water in place. So initially if you feel like you are drinking masses more water but seem to be peeing an awful lot too, then it could be that some EFA's are needed to balance the water, to help hold it in your body, so that it can be absorbed. Linseeds can help massively with this and soaking linseeds overnight as mentioned above and then drinking the water along with the seeds on a daily basis first thing each morning for a few weeks will really help to address this imbalance and help to bring your body more into alignment. Other EFA's can also be found in oily fish such as salmon, sardines and anchovies and also in avocados, olive oil and cod liver oil. So introducing more of these into your diet may help too.

Final note –

Being in a state of good and vibrant health comes from healthy living. By making healthy choices we can begin working towards restoring balance to the body. The ideal is to reach a state of equilibrium or homeostasis where all of the body systems are functioning optimally so we can then feel at our best. The human body knows how to heal itself if given the right environment and the tools to do so. Poor health therefore is just the body being out of balance and we can do so much to change this.

So, basically, that's all there is to achieving Easy and Effective Enemas! So simple to do and yet so amazingly powerful! I hope that you have found this guide useful and that you enjoy the process of doing your own enemas at home or wherever you choose to do them and more importantly, I really do hope that you enjoy better health by regularly taking them.

Wishing you greater health and happiness

Susie x

www.creatingbalance.uk

IMPORTANT CONTRAINDICATIONS – Enemas should not be performed during pregnancy or while trying to get pregnant.

Also please remember that although it is very safe to do an enema, just be a little more careful and gentle if you have haemorrhoids.

SUGGESTED SUPPLIERS AND REFERENCES –

Enema kits – From online shops or local chemists

For chickweed cream there are many companies online.

Almond oil – from chemists and good quality health food shops or online.

Waterproof pads and mats – Disabled stores, baby shops or some department stores.

Germ-a-clenz – Tigon raw wild supplements. www.oliveleaf.co.uk – family owned business selling natural good quality products.

Natural body care products – www.houseofmistry.com

The Flax Farm in the UK – are a very good source for quality flax oil. Flax oil can be found in some health food shops and supermarkets. It is always best to get cold pressed oil in a dark glass bottle so that it is protected from the light and heat.

Essential Oils – Doterra sell lovely quality oils.

Foot stools/stepping stools – Internet, baby/children's stores

Probiotics and good gut support with high quality health products – www.gutdoctor.com

To find a colonic therapist in the UK try – www.colonic-association.org

RECOMMENDED FURTHER READING –

For additional reading and interest, I thoroughly recommend the following books to help further improve your health –

Your Bodies Many Cries for Water – F. Batmanghelidj M.D.

The Hidden Messages in Water – Masaru Emoto

Detox your world – Shazzie – This is a great book covering many basic aspects of health and wellness.

*Let That Sh*t Go*! – 31 things to do if you want a better poo! – Katherine Brooke-Mackenzie

Love your Liver Feel Alive – Susan Laing

Digestive Health – Philip Day

Natural Born Healer – Lucy De Angeles

ABOUT THE AUTHOR –

Susie initially trained in secretarial work, but came to study nutrition and naturopathic principles after experiencing the power of using natural therapies and dietary changes while healing her own serious skin condition in 2004. She was inspired to train with the Nutritional Healing Foundation and also with Hippocrates Health Institute in Florida where she learnt the importance of enemas as part of a healing programme. She also has qualifications in Emotional Freedom Technique (EFT) and Reiki.

ACKNOWLEDGEMENTS –

A huge thank you and much appreciation to my wonderful family and friends who have offered their support as well as encouragement while I have been writing this book.

A JOURNEY OF CHANGE

They say that it takes just 21 days to break a habit, or to form a new one. If this is true, then by taking consistent steps every day for 21 days and beyond, there is great potential for creating more balance in your body and to feeling much healthier.

The following 21 pages of quotes are an opportunity for you to record your own 21 day 'Journey of change' along with some ideas to get you started.

"The doctor of the future will give no medicine, but will instruct his patients in care of the human frame, in diet and in the cause and prevention of disease" - Thomas Edison

* Drink more quality fresh water. Try starting with a mug of water and a slice of lemon or ginger first thing in the morning.

"Prevention is better than cure" - Desiderius Erasmus

* Go to bed an hour or two earlier to reap the benefits both in energy and extra time in the mornings.

"Take care of your body, it's the only place you have to live"
- Jim Rohn

* Try food combining - Eating carbohydrate meals (such as bread, pasta, potatoes or rice) separately to protein meals (such as chicken or fish) can improve digestion, assimilation and weight loss.

"*Self care is how you take your power back*" - Lala Delia

* Turn devices off early in the evening for a more restful sleep. If phones need to be in the bedroom, then at least have them in flight mode.

"Your body holds deep wisdom, trust in it, learn from it, nourish it, watch your life transformation and be healthy" - Bella Bleue

* Walk more! - walking before a meal triggers metabolism and walking after a meal helps digestion, so both are good.

"Health is like money, we never have a true idea of its value until we lose it"

* On bright sunny days throw open the windows for extra oxygen and to stay more alert.

"Family, Nature and Health all go together" - Olivia Newton John

* Sleeping with windows open at night prevents that stuffy head in the morning!

"All the money in the world can't buy back good health"
- Reba McEntire

* Add a side salad to all your main meals or replace the lunch time sandwich with a salad. If you nourish your body, you nourish your mind so you feel better.

"Good health is the best insurance policy"

* Wearing natural fibres such as cotton, linen or wool and sleeping in 100% cotton or silk bedding helps your skin to breathe!

"A healthy outside starts from the inside" - Robert Urich

* Try probiotics for 30 days to help increase healthy bacteria and flora. Your immune system gets a boost when you do this. (NB. If you need to take a course of antibiotics, then following with a course of probiotics helps to repopulate the gut flora, as antibiotics unfortunately knock out both the good as well as the bad bacteria).

"A good laugh and a long sleep are the best cures in the doctors book" - Irish proverb

* Start a new hobby. Is there something you've always fancied doing but never gotten around to, like learning a new language or maybe starting a dance class? There are so many options to try.

"You've got to nourish to flourish!" - Chloe Myers

* Switch normal tea and coffee for either Green tea, Rooibos, or other herbal teas. Or cut down to just 1 or 2 cups of organic tea and good quality coffee per day.

“Looking after my health today gives me a better hope for tomorrow” - Anne Wilson Schaef

* Cut down on sugar. Use natural sweeteners such as honey, molasses, coconut sugar, maple syrup or add dried fruit to recipes.

"The art of healing comes from nature, not from the physician. Therefore the physician must start from nature, with an open mind" - Paracelsus

* Spending time in nature, at the beach, by the river, or in the woods helps you to feel uplifted and more connected to your spirit, which in this fast paced life is very much needed!

"We need to have healthcare as opposed to sick care"

* Try intermittent fasting. The goal is to eat within a smaller window. So you only eat between say 12pm and 6pm. Build up slowly, narrowing the gap day by day until you reach a 5 or 6 hour window. By doing this your body has a chance to rest from digestion and can focus on house cleaning, repairing and regenerating cells, enabling you to have more energy, vitality and longevity.

"Healthy citizens are the greatest asset any country can have"
- Sir Winston Churchill

* Replace normal table salt with natural sea salt or Celtic salt which contain valuable minerals. Adding seaweeds such as dulce, kelp and nori to foods gives extra minerals and a salty flavour.

"Sleep is that golden chain that ties health and our bodies together"
- Thomas Dekker

* Eating a rainbow of colourful fruit, vegetables and herbs
supply your body with vitamins, minerals, phytonutrients and
antioxidants, which help to reduce the free radicals
and protect you from diseases such as cancer and heart disease.
Nutrition is the fundamental building block to health.

"I find it a lot healthier to be some place where I can go outside in my bare feet" - James Taylor

* Relaxation is so important for your emotional well-being. Meditation, yoga, listening to calming music, sunbathing, an afternoon nap, a gentle walk, getting lost in a good book or a hobby that you love will help you to switch off from the stresses of daily life.

"I believe the greatest gift you can give your family and the world is a healthy You!" - Joyce Meyer

* Grounding has become very popular in recent years. Placing bare feet onto the earth, grass, or sand for a few minutes is very calming and helps to restore balance in your body and relieve stress.

"You can have all the riches in the world, but if you don't have your health, you have nothing" - Steven Adler

* Sweating via saunas, epsom salt baths, vigorous exercise, infrared saunas are all helpful ways to encourage the release of toxins via the skin.

"Let food be thy medicine and medicine be thy food" - Hippocrates

* Remember these S's for extra nutrition and interest - Smoothies, Soups, Stews, Salads, Stocks (especially from bones). Seeds - Sunflower, Sesame etc. Sprouted seeds. Spices.

TRICORN
BOOKS

Printed in Great Britain
by Amazon

42816168R00043